EXTREME SPORTS

BMX

by Tracy Vonder Brink

I0811453

pogo

Ideas for Parents and Teachers

Pogo Books let children practice reading informational text while introducing them to nonfiction features such as headings, labels, sidebars, maps, and diagrams, as well as a table of contents, glossary, and index.

Carefully leveled text with a strong photo match offers early fluent readers the support they need to succeed.

Before Reading

- "Walk" through the book and point out the various nonfiction features. Ask the student what purpose each feature serves.
- Look at the glossary together. Read and discuss the words.

Read the Book

- Have the child read the book independently.
- Invite them to list questions that arise from reading.

After Reading

- Discuss the child's questions. Talk about how they might find answers to those questions.
- Prompt the child to think more. Ask: Would you like to try BMX? Why or why not?

Pogo Books are published by Jump!
5357 Penn Avenue South
Minneapolis, MN 55419
www.jumplibrary.com

Copyright © 2025 Jump!
International copyright reserved in all countries.
No part of this book may be reproduced in any form without written permission from the publisher.

Library of Congress Cataloging-in-Publication Data

Names: Vonder Brink, Tracy, author.
Title: BMX / by Tracy Vonder Brink.
Description: Minneapolis, MN: Jump!, Inc., [2025]
Series: Extreme sports | Includes index.
Audience: Ages 7-10
Identifiers: LCCN 2024026104 (print)
LCCN 2024026105 (ebook)
ISBN 9798892136334 (hardcover)
ISBN 9798892136341 (paperback)
ISBN 9798892136358 (ebook)
Subjects: LCSH: Bicycle motocross–Juvenile literature.
BMX freestyle (Stunt cycling)–Juvenile literature.
Classification: LCC GV1049.3 .V66 2025 (print)
LCC GV1049.3 (ebook)
DDC 796.6/22–dc23/eng/20240629
LC record available at https://lccn.loc.gov/2024026104
LC ebook record available at https://lccn.loc.gov/2024026105

Editor: Alyssa Sorenson
Designer: Molly Ballanger
Content Consultant: Karl Clark, Black Mountain BMX Raceway

Photo Credits: Konrad Swierad/Shutterstock, cover; MarcelClemens/Shutterstock, 1, 12-13; Chbm89/Dreamstime, 3; ATTILA KISBENEDEK/Getty, 4; Al Bello/Getty, 5; homydesign/Shutterstock, 6-7tl; tsuyoshi_kinjyo/iStock, 6-7tr; Aitor Lamadrid/Dreamstime, 6-7bl; Mikel Taboada/Shutterstock, 6-7br; Danredrup/Dreamstime, 8-9 (top); Rudolf Ernst/Dreamstime, 8-9 (bottom); Homydesign/Dreamstime, 10; Francois Nel/Getty, 11; Saravut Biacharas/Dreamstime, 14-15; ANDY BUCHANAN/AFP/Getty, 16; SeventyFour/Shutterstock, 17; WANG ZHAO/AFP/Getty, 18-19; Matt Fowler KC/Shutterstock, 19; Stanislav Kogiku/SOPA Images/LightRocket/Getty, 20-21; Eric Alexandre/Shutterstock, 23.

Printed in the United States of America at Corporate Graphics in North Mankato, Minnesota.

TABLE OF CONTENTS

CHAPTER 1

LET'S RIDE!

A BMX rider zooms up a ramp on her bike. She reaches the top of the ramp. She is in the air!

She loops into a backflip. How? She uses **physics** and the right equipment!

racing

park

dirt

street

Racing and freestyle are two kinds of BMX. Racing involves riding around a track. In freestyle, riders do tricks with their bikes.

Park, dirt, and street are three kinds of freestyle. In park, riders do jumps and tricks at skate parks. Dirt riders do them on a dirt track. Street riders do them in public places.

DID YOU KNOW?

BMX stands for "bicycle motocross." Motocross is a kind of motorcycle race. People started BMX in the 1970s. They wanted to race their bikes like motorcycles.

Different kinds of BMX need different bikes. A racing bike is made with lightweight metal. Why? The bike is light. It takes less **energy** for a rider to move.

Freestyle bikes are heavier. They must be **sturdy**. They help riders land tricks safely.

DID YOU KNOW?

Riders wear helmets. They also wear long-sleeved shirts, pants, and gloves when they race. These protect them if they fall.

racing

freestyle

CHAPTER 2

OFF TO THE RACES

Racers take off! They speed around a track. They stand on their pedals. Why? This lets them use more strength from their hips and legs to push harder. They use this **force** to go faster.

They speed into the first **berm**. The bikes lean as riders take the curve. The riders lean their shoulders the other way. Why? This changes their **center of gravity**. It keeps them balanced and their bikes from falling over.

Next, riders race up a small hill. The hill acts as a ramp. It lets riders launch their bikes into a jump! **Gravity** pulls the bikes back to the ground.

DID YOU KNOW?

Riders keep their knees bent when landing. Why? It helps their legs **absorb** energy. This makes the landing softer. It helps prevent injuries.

Next is the rhythm section. Riders **pump** as they go over the jumps. This helps them gain **momentum**. They go fast. The finish line is close!

TAKE A LOOK!

How does pumping work? Take a look!

1 **A rider approaches a jump. They center their body on the bike.**

2 **The rider goes up a jump. They lift their legs, shoulders, and arms up.**

3 **The front wheel goes over the jump. The rider pushes their legs, shoulders, and arms down and forward. This builds momentum.**

CHAPTER 3

FREESTYLE FUN

Some freestyle bikes have pegs. Pegs stick out from the wheels. A rider stands on a peg to do a trick. This helps her center her weight. Now she can balance on one wheel!

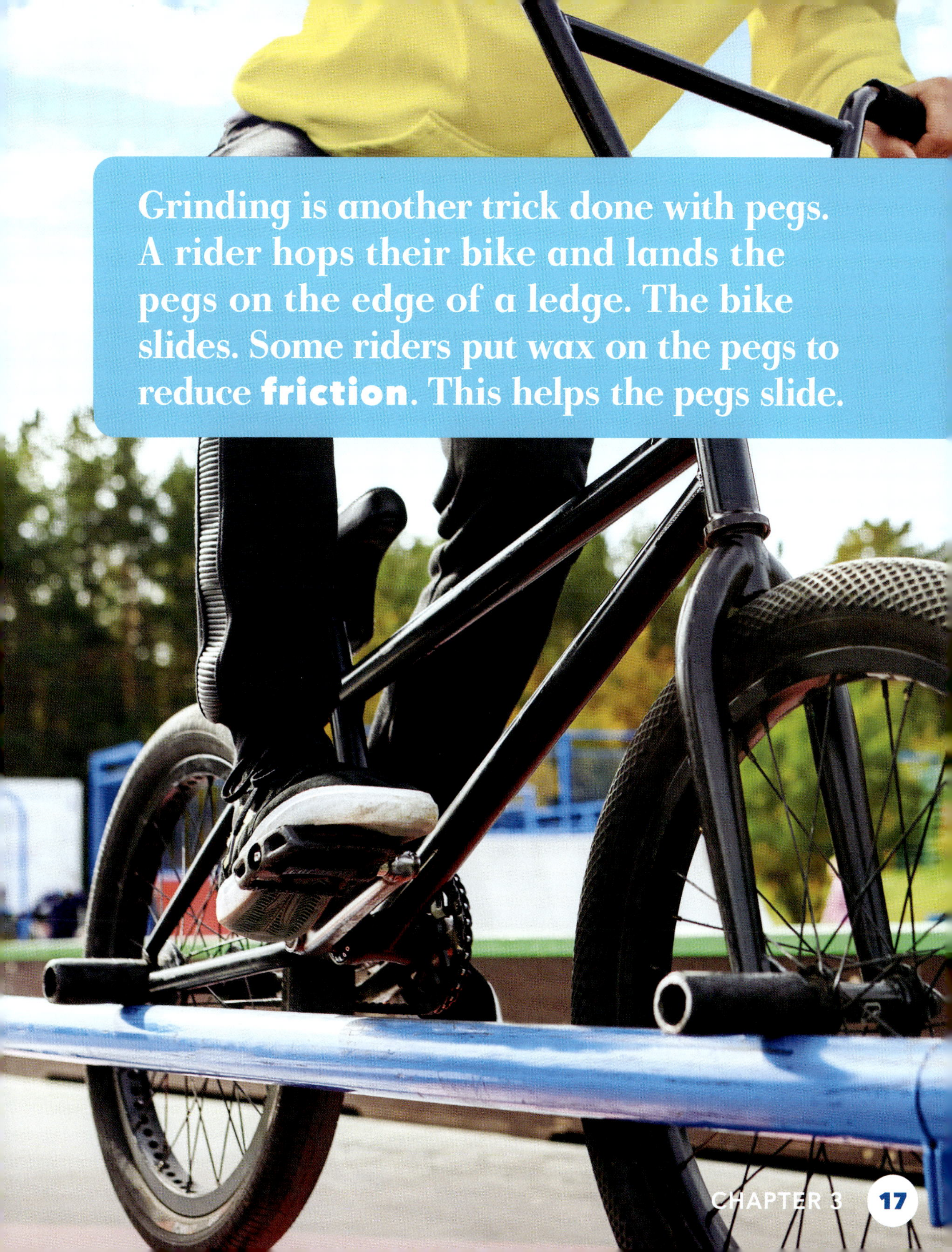

Grinding is another trick done with pegs. A rider hops their bike and lands the pegs on the edge of a ledge. The bike slides. Some riders put wax on the pegs to reduce **friction**. This helps the pegs slide.

IMAX
KIA

Another rider pedals across a U-shaped ramp. This helps build momentum. The rider leans back as the front wheel reaches the top. The rider **rotates** with the bike. They do a backflip!

The Superman trick also uses momentum. The rider takes his feet off the pedals as the bike leaves the ramp. He snaps his legs backward. He pushes his arms forward. Momentum keeps his bike and body moving through the air. He looks like a flying superhero!

The best BMX riders **compete** at the Olympics and the X Games. Understanding how to use their bikes and their bodies helps them win!

SHADOW SERPENT

ACTIVITIES & TOOLS

TRY THIS!

CENTER OF GRAVITY

Your center of gravity keeps you balanced. It changes depending on how you move. See how it works with this fun activity!

What You Need:

- a wall

1. Stand up straight next to a wall. Your center of gravity is around your belly button.
2. Stand with your right leg and shoulder touching the wall.
3. Try to raise your left leg and stand on your right leg.
4. What do you notice? It is impossible! Why? To stay balanced, your center of gravity needs to be over your right foot. But the wall is in the way.
5. Move away from the wall. Try raising your left leg again. Where is your center of gravity now? How does it keep you balanced?

GLOSSARY

absorb: To take in.

berm: A sloped turn.

center of gravity: The point on an object at which half of its weight is on one side and half is on the other.

compete: To try to win a contest.

energy: The ability or strength to do things without getting tired.

force: Something that causes an object to move or change its speed or direction.

friction: The force that slows down objects when they rub against each other.

gravity: The force that pulls things toward the center of Earth and keeps them from floating away.

momentum: The force or speed something gains as it moves.

physics: The science that deals with matter, energy, and their interactions.

pump: A BMX racing technique used to gain speed over jumps.

rotates: Turns around a center point.

sturdy: Built strong and able to last.

INDEX

TO LEARN MORE

Finding more information is as easy as 1, 2, 3.

1. Go to www.factsurfer.com
2. Enter "BMX" into the search box.
3. Choose your book to see a list of websites.

FACT SURFER